George Washington Julian

The Rank of Charles Osborn as an Anti-Slavery Pioneer

George Washington Julian

The Rank of Charles Osborn as an Anti-Slavery Pioneer

ISBN/EAN: 9783744732215

Printed in Europe, USA, Canada, Australia, Japan

Cover: Foto ©ninafisch / pixelio.de

More available books at **www.hansebooks.com**

THE RANK

OF

CHARLES OSBORN

AS AN

ANTI-SLAVERY PIONEER.

BY

GEORGE W. JULIAN.

INDIANAPOLIS:
THE BOWEN-MERRILL COMPANY.
1891.

INDIANA HISTORICAL SOCIETY

HON. W. H. ENGLISH, PRESIDENT.
GEN. JOHN COBURN, 1ST VICE-PRESIDENT.
WM. W. WOOLLEN, 2D VICE-PRES. AND COR. SECRETARY.
JUDGE D. W. HOWE, 3D VICE-PRESIDENT.
W. DEM. HOOPER, TREASURER.
J. P. DUNN, JR., RECORDING SECRETARY.

INDIANA HISTORICAL SOCIETY PAMPHLETS

No. 1. **The Laws and Courts of Northwest and Indiana Territories.** By Daniel Waite Howe.

No. 2. **The Life and Services of John B. Dillon.** By Gen. John Coburn and Judge Horace P. Biddle.

No. 3. **The Acquisition of Louisiana.** By Judge Thomas M. Cooley.

No. 4. **Loughery's Defeat and Pigeon Roost Massacre.** By Charles Martindale.

No. 5. **A Descriptive Catalogue of the Official Publications of the Territory and State of Indiana from 1800 to 1890.** By Daniel Waite Howe.

No. 6. **The Rank of Charles Osborn as an Anti-Slavery Pioneer.** By George W. Julian.

These pamphlets are printed and sold for the benefit of the Indiana Historical Society. It is the purpose of the Society to publish, from time to time, other original papers, and to reprint rare and valuable documents relating to the history of the State. With a view to the general circulation of its publications, they will be issued in cheap form, the price charged for them being for the purpose of defraying the expense of publication.

A. L. ROACHE, W. DEM. HOOPER,
A. C. HARRIS, J. P. DUNN, JR.,
J. R. WILSON.

Executive Committee.

Published and Sold by

THE BOWEN-MERRILL CO.

INDIANAPOLIS, IND.

INDIANA HISTORICAL SOCIETY PUBLICATIONS.

VOLUME II.   NUMBER 6.

THE RANK

OF

CHARLES OSBORN

AS AN

ANTI-SLAVERY PIONEER.

BY

GEORGE W. JULIAN.

INDIANAPOLIS:
THE BOWEN-MERRILL COMPANY.
1891.

In the *International Review* for June, 1882, I endeavored to show the unfaithfulness of current history in dealing with the genesis of modern abolitionism, and that justice has been strangely denied to a faithful anti-slavery pioneer who was a citizen of Indiana during the latter part of his long life. In the number of this *Review* for September following, Mr. Oliver Johnson earnestly combated my positions, and the controversy was closed by my rejoinder in the number for November. The question discussed is full of historic interest, and in the following paper I have dealt with it more fully, and, I think, conclusively. I respectfully submit my views to our State Historical Society as a slight contribution to the work it has in charge.

G. W. J.

CHARLES OSBORN.

In just so far as the interests of humanity transcend those of country and race the philanthropists and reformers who devoted their lives and fortunes to the overthrow of American slavery are more worthy of honor than the patriots who toiled for national independence and the liberty of white men. It is therefore gratifying to notice the steadily growing disposition in all directions to do fitting honor to the pioneers and heroes of the anti-slavery struggle in the United States. Oliver Johnson's book, entitled "Garrison and the Anti-Slavery Movement," has appeared in a second edition, and is charmingly written by an intimate friend and fellow-laborer in the cause, who naturally displays his unbounded admiration for its great moral leader. A far more voluminous life of Mr. Garrison has since been given to the public by his children, which is also an admirable history of the great movement of which he was so long the recognized head. Elizur Wright, himself an able, faithful and time-honored pioneer, prepared and published a few years ago an interesting sketch of Myron Holley, one of the earliest leaders and champions of organized political action against slavery, and a man of singular rectitude, ability, courage and eloquence. Hon. E. B. Washburne is the author of a well-deserved life of Edward Coles, the anti-slavery governor of Illinois, who successfully resisted the establishment of slavery in that state, in the years 1823-24, by a scheme of organized border ruffianism akin to that which in later years came so near making Kansas a slave state. General William Birney has just honored himself by publishing a life of his father, James G. Birney, the distinguished leader of the Liberty party and its candidate for president in 1840 and 1844. There is yet wanting an adequate life of Benjamin Lundy, whose perfect disinterestedness, self-denying zeal and absolute devotion to humanity entitle him to the highest place on the calendar of anti-slavery pioneers. Still other lives are yet to be written, and although a trustworthy history of the anti-slavery movement can not be expected till we are further from the strifes and passions with which it was unavoidably connected, yet it is not too soon to insist upon justice and fair play in dealing with its real founders and apostles.

Our accepted histories and manuals agree in according to William Lloyd Garrison the honor of first proclaiming, on this side of the Atlantic, the doctrine of "immediate and unconditional emancipation." They also agree in awarding to Benjamin Lundy the credit of publishing the first anti-slavery newspaper of this century, and of being the pioneer abolitionist of the United States. These statements are now received without question, and supported by Johnson's "Life of Garrison," Greeley's "History of the American Conflict," Wilson's "History of the Rise and Fall of the Slave Power," Von Holst's "Constitutional and Political History of the United States," and various other authorities. It is the chief purpose of this paper to controvert these alleged facts, and to show that Charles Osborn, an eminent minister in the Society of Friends, proclaimed the doctrine of immediate and unconditional emancipation when William Lloyd Garrison was only nine years old, and nearly a dozen years before that doctrine was announced by Elizabeth Heyrick, in England; and that Mr. Osborn also edited and published one of the first anti-slavery newspapers in the United States, and is thus entitled to take rank as the real pioneer of American abolitionism. These statements may appear surprising, but, if true, they should be so recognized. If the current of history has been diverted into a false channel, it should be turned into the true one. The story of the great conflict should be made thoroughly accurate and trustworthy. When a great victory has been won, every general should have his due share in the honor of its achievement, and, if the heroism of any brave man has been slighted, and the fact can be shown by newly discovered evidence, the record of the battle should be made to conform to the truth. It can scarcely be necessary to say that I have no desire whatever to do the slightest injustice to Garrison and Lundy. Their exalted place as heroes in the grand army of human progress is irreversibly established; and Garrison and Lundy themselves, if living, would be the last to deny to a fellow-laborer in the great cause the share of honor he had fairly earned in its service.

Before proceeding with my task, let me briefly sketch the principal facts of the life of Charles Osborn. It appears, from the published journal of his travels, that he was born in North Carolina, on the 21st of August, 1775. In his nineteenth year he removed to Tennessee, where he made his first appearance in the ministry about the year 1806. He soon took rank as a preacher of considerable gifts, and traveled and preached extensively in North Carolina and Tennessee, taking an active part in the anti-slavery societies of these States. He removed to Mount Pleasant, Ohio, in 1816, where he published a religious and reformatory newspaper, and continued his work in the ministry. In 1819 he settled in Indiana. He took an active and leading part, as an orthodox Friend, in the movement against Elias Hicks and his followers, and after this made a religious visit to Great Britain and a part of the continent. He sat at the head of the yearly meetings of this country for about the third of a century, and the like honor was accorded him, though unsought, by Friends on the other side of the Atlantic during his sojourn among them. From his earliest years he was known as a thorough-going abolitionist, and an abstainer from the use of slave-grown produce; and, in his later life, he became involved in a controversy with his society on the slavery question, which resulted in his separation from it in testimony of his unflinching devotion to the slave.

Respecting Mr. Osborn's connection with the doctrine of immediate and unconditional emancipation, I submit the following facts:

1. In the month of December, 1814, he took the lead in organizing the "Tennessee Manumission Society." It was formed at the house of Elihu Swain, his father-in-law, and its object was the immediate and unconditional manumission of the slaves. Rachel Swain, now known as Rachel Davis, a daughter of Elihu Swain, still survives, and resides in Wayne county, Indiana, and she says she was present at the organization of the society, and knows the facts I have stated. I have personally known her many years, and know her to be an entirely trustworthy witness. It is true she is now very old, and the facts to which she bears witness happened a long time ago; but while the memory of old people touching recent events is very untrustworthy it is vivid as to those of childhood and early life. Moreover, her statements are corroborated by persons still living, whose names I shall presently mention, and who form a connecting link between that early period and the present. From them I learn the character of the first manumission societies of Tennessee and North Carolina. Their mission was not political but moral. Slavery had not then found its way into politics. Their appeal was to the individual. Like the Garrisonian abolitionists of a later day they taught the sinfulness of slavery and the duty

of immediate repentance. Let me add that in 1852, when Mrs. Davis was only fifty years old, she united with the Society of Anti-Slavery Friends, of which she was then a member in witness of the facts she now affirms.

2. My second witness is Rev. John Rankin, a native of Tennessee, where he resided till the year 1817. He then removed to Kentucky, and afterwards to Ohio, where he died a few years ago, at the age of ninety-odd years. Few men are more widely known to the anti-slavery public. He founded the Western Tract Society, at Cincinnati, for the purpose of supplying the country with anti-slavery information. He was one of the first lecturers sent out by the American Anti-Slavery Society, of which he was also one of the founders. As preacher, writer and lecturer, he was most honorably known. He was an uncompromising abolitionist from his youth up, and he preached his doctrines boldly from the pulpit at a very early day, both in the South and in the North. He says the manumission society referred to proclaimed the doctrine of immediate emancipation, and that after his removal to Kentucky he proclaimed it to large congregations. In 1824, after his removal to Ohio, he published a series of letters setting forth the sinfulness of slave-holding, and avowing the same principle. These letters were published in book form in 1825, and were printed in the *Liberator*. That Mr. Garrison was well pleased with the book is shown by the following inscription on the fly-leaf of a volume of his own writings, which he presented to Mr. Rankin:

"Rev. John Rankin, with the profound regards and loving veneration of his anti-slavery disciple and humble co-worker in the cause of emancipation, William Lloyd Garrison."

To this evidence of Mr. Rankin I now add that of his brother, Dr. A. T. Rankin, who has recently made the

public statement that John Rankin preached immediate
and unconditional emancipation as early as the year 1817.
His letters to me on the subject, with those of his brother,
are before me. It should be remembered, also, that according to the first volumne of Henry Wilson's "History
of slavery," page 178, at a meeting of the American Anti-
Slavery Society in New York, years ago, John Rankin
made the same statement respecting his early and public
espousal of immediate emancipation.

But I do not rest the case here, and shall show the trust-
worthiness of Mr. Rankin's recollection by his letters
already referred to, written in the year 1824, and published in book form the year following. As an arraign-
ment of slavery this book is as terrible as it is just. He
shows it to be a curse to both master and slave, a horrid
conspiracy against marriage and the family, an outrage
upon the inborn rights of man, a blight and a blast upon
every community in which it exists, a loathsome mockery
of the very principle of free government, and a palpable
violation of the express law of God. The writer of such
a book who religiously believed what he wrote, as did
John Rankin, could never have tolerated the thought of
postponing the duty of emancipation for a day or an hour.
But putting aside the general character of the book, I
propose to remove all doubt or cavil by particular extracts
from its pages. I quote from page 34 of the third edition,
printed at Newburyport, Massachusetts:

"And here I must remark upon one main objection to
the emancipation of the slaves: it is that they are, in con-
sequence of the want of information, incapacitated for
freedom, and that it is necessary to detain them in bondage until they may be better prepared for liberation. But
from the preceding remarks it is abundantly evident that
they are now better prepared with respect to information
for emancipation than they will be at any future period,

and that less inconvenience and danger would attend their liberation at present than at any future time. It must be obvious to every one capable of discernment that the inconvenience and danger of emancipation will increase in proportion as slaves become more numerous. Indeed, all the difficulties that attend emancipation are rapidly increasing, and they must certainly be endured at some period, sooner or later; for it is most absurd to imagine that such an immense body of people, most rapidly increasing, can always be detained in bondage, and, therefore, it is much better to endure those difficulties *now* than it will be when they shall have grown to the most enormous size."

I quote also the following on page 116:

"We are commanded to do justly and love mercy, and this we ought to do without delay, and leave the consequences attending it to the control of Him who gave the command. We ought also to remember that no excuse for disobedience will avail anything when He shall call us to judgment."

If this does not clearly inculcate the duty of immediate emancipation, words have no meaning or were made to deceive. The reasonableness and credibility of Mr. Rankin's statement are made evident by some kindred facts, and I refer to them for the purpose of still further showing how completely mistaken are those who assume that nobody in this country announced the doctrine in question prior to Mr. Garrison, in 1829. In 1824 Rev. James Duncan proclaimed it in his book entitled "A Treatise on Slavery." In December, 1825, Lundy published in the *Genius of Universal Emancipation*, Elizabeth Heyrick's famous pamphlet, "Immediate, not Gradual Emancipation." In the same issue of the paper I find a vigorous article, in which the principle is clearly asserted and argued. The name of the writer does not appear, because the article seems to be one of a series, and I have not been able to find the preceding and following issues of the paper. I quote the following passage:

"The slave has a *right* to his liberty—a right which it is a crime to withhold—let the consequences to the planters be what they may. * * * The cause of emancipation calls for something more decisive, more efficient, than words. It calls upon the real friends of the poor, degraded African to bind themselves by a solemn engagement, an irreversible vow, to participate no longer in the crime of keeping him in bondage."

The same doctrine is declared, with still greater precision and emphasis, in an article published in the *Genius* for August 5, 1826. It bears evidence of having been written by a Presbyterian minister. After insisting that slavery is a crime, he says:

"What has God told you about crime, or sin? To desist from it, or persevere? To desist. When? Now! Now!! Yes, mortal, He never gave man or angel a moment to consider—a minute to wait for the alteration of affairs, or for more favorable circumstances. If we are required to do right, we are required to do it immediately."

The subject of immediate emancipation is likewise discussed in the *Genius* for October, 1822, by Benjamin Lundy himself, in reply to a writer who has inveighed against the terrible consequences which would result from it, thus showing that the idea was then in the minds of men. Mr. Garrison, in all probability, read the articles to which I have referred at the time of their appearance, as he had read Rankin's book; but whether he did or not I have made it certain that he was not first in announcing the principle of immediate emancipation in this country.

3. In the year 1841 Mr. Osborn, as I shall hereafter have occasion to show, gave offense to his society by his earnest and uncompromising espousal of the doctrine in question;

and the well-known Levi Coffin, in his published volume of "Reminiscences," on page 231, referring to that period, says that Mr. Osborn "preached no new doctrine, had experienced no change, but followed the same course and advocated the same anti-slavery doctrine he had for forty years." He further says, on page 265, that he publicly advocated immediate and unconditional emancipation in Ohio in 1816. Mr. Coffin knew him in his youth, and gave these testimonies from his personal knowledge. As a philanthropist Mr. Coffin is very widely known and worthily remembered. His devotion to humanity was a passion, while in the matter of integrity he was as guileless as a little child. It will not do to say that his old age weakens the value of his testimony; for although he was an old man when he wrote his "Reminiscences," he had given the same evidence, as I shall show, in the year 1843, when in the prime of life, and only removed some twenty-odd years from the time when Mr. Osborn's manumission society in Tennessee was formed. He is a competent and credible witness, and his evidence must be accepted as true or successfully impeached.

4. In a printed document published in 1843, reviewing certain proceedings of the Indiana yearly meeting in dealing with Mr. Osborn, the following statement is made: "It is well known that the sentiments of Charles Osborn in relation to this subject (slavery) are the same now they were more than twenty-five years ago." This is signed by Daniel Puckett, Walter Edgerton, H. H. Way, Jacob Graves, John Shugart, and Levi Coffin—all perfectly reliable men, and three of them, namely, Puckett, Way and Coffin, were intimately acquainted with Mr. Osborn and his anti-slavery position during the period covering his life and labors in Tennessee and North Carolina. I personally know all these to have been perfectly trustworthy witnesses and intelligent men. They were leaders in the religious

society to which they belonged, and none of them were then beyond the meridian of life.

5. After the death of Mr. Osborn a memorial of his life was drawn up and adopted by the Society of Anti-Slavery Friends, to which he belonged, in March, 1852. That memorial refers to his leadership in the formation of manumission societies in 1814, and declares that, "in endeavoring to lay the foundation principle of these societies, he, at that early day, advocated and maintained the only true and Christian ground—immediate and unconditional emancipation." After this memorial was drawn it was submitted to the monthly meeting, and, according to the practice in all such cases, was scrutinized before its approval. It then had to be sent to the quarterly meeting, composed of the members of the different monthly meetings, and again examined and passed. It was then forwarded to the meeting for sufferings, composed of representatives from each of the quarterly meetings, composing the yearly meeting, and a certain number to represent the latter. This body of men again examined and approved it, after which it was read in the yearly meeting before the members of the society, *en masse*, who approved and adopted it. In these several meetings were such men as Levi Coffin, William Beard, Henry H. Way, Enoch Macy, Jonathan Swain, Thomas Frazier, Daniel Puckett, Isaiah Osborn, William Hough, Walter Edgerton, Benjamin Stanton, John Shugart, Jacob Graves, and various others, many of whom were personally and intimately acquainted with Charles Osborn and his labors in the manumission cause in Tennessee and North Carolina. They were men of the highest character for integrity, and could not have been induced to sit by and approve statements about which they were well informed if they were false. In my earlier life I knew all these men, and I entertain not the shadow of a doubt as to the perfect accuracy of their statements.

6. The manumission movement in Tennessee awakened uneasiness among the slave-holders, some of whom thought it would be good policy to attach themselves to it as members. In a moment of weakness, and on considerations of expediency, the constitution of the society was so changed as to permit this; and this led to a further compromise, by which the name of the society was changed to that of "Manumission and Colonization Society." Mr. Osborn was present when these changes were proposed and adopted, and gave them his decided opposition. In the language of the Quakers of a later day, he believed "the full enjoyment of liberty to be the right of all, without any conditions," and could not "consent, upon any conditions, that the bondage of a fellow-being shall be prolonged for a single day," nor "say to him he must go to Hayti, to Liberia, or any other place, to entitle him to the full enjoyment of liberty." The facts respecting these changes in the policy of the manumission movement and Mr. Osborn's opposition are given on the authority of his early friends and anti-slavery associates, already referred to, and are more particularly set forth in Edgerton's "History of the Separation in Indiana Yearly Meeting of Friends," published in 1856, and in Mr. Osborn's "Journal of His Travels and Labors in the Ministry," published in 1854.

7. In enumerating these proofs I ought to make more special and emphatic mention of Mr. Osborn's hostility to African colonization. He avowed this in his youth, and never afterward faltered. The fact is as honorable to him as it is remarkable that, while the leading abolitionists of England and the United States were caught in this snare, he was never for a moment deluded by any of its plausibilities. His moral vision detected its character from the beginning. "Emancipation," he declared, "was thrown into the cradle of colonization, there to be rocked and

kept quiet until the last slave-holder should become willing to send his human chattels to the colony." Benjamin Lundy and other anti-slavery men discussed it as a scheme of gradual emancipation, and as such Mr. Osborn always understood it. He opposed it because it postponed the freedom of the slaves and placed conditions in its way. This subtle scheme of imposture and inhumanity became a national organization in the beginning of the year 1817, and became at once the great stalking-horse of slavery. It darkened the air, palsied the public conscience, and balked all efforts looking to immediate emancipation. It draped over the abomination of slavery, and debauched the judgment of the country. Like Aaron's rod, it swallowed up all else. It was the grand stumbling-block of philanthropy, and the colossal falsehood of the generation. There was but one thing for a thoroughly earnest anti-slavery man to do, and that was to fight it. This Mr. Osborn did, single-handed. He girded himself for battle against the most formidable and insidious foe of freedom that had ever stood in its path. He was a *doer* of the word from his youth, and I have a right to define his position by the unambiguous testimony of his life.

It is not pretended, of course, that Mr. Osborn expected that the slave-holders would immediately emancipate their slaves. Without the intervention of a miracle this was impossible. The work of emancipation could only go forward under the inevitable conditions by which it was complicated. It had to become an educational process before it could be realized in fact. This was Mr. Garrison's idea, for he had no thought of emancipation by force. What Mr. Osborn preached to the slave-holder was the doctrine of immediate repentance, and that he had no right to put off that repentance to a more convenient season. That was his well-known position in 1830, when

the anti-slavery agitation began seriously to disturb the
peace of the country; and the Indiana yearly meeting,
which could not endure this doctrine in 1842, never disputed the fact that he had at all times avowed it. If it be
said that it was well known that the honor of first proclaiming this doctrine in this country was ascribed to Mr. Garrison by his friends, and that Mr. Osborn would have contested this claim if he had felt himself entitled to make it,
I reply that he was a traveling minister among Friends,
engrossed in his peculiar work, and may have known
nothing of the matter. It is quite as reasonable to suppose
him ignorant of the claim made by the friends of Mr. Garrison as to suppose the latter ignorant of Mr. Osborn's
well-known record as an immediate emancipationist. In
justice to him it should also be said that he was too modest to blow his own trumpet, and too much absorbed in his
work to concern himself about its honors; and that if this
had been otherwise he had no motive to enter into any
strife over the question. The champions of immediate
emancipation, when it first began to stir the country, and
during the life of Mr. Osborn, were obliged to make themselves of no reputation. They were cast out of all the
synagogues of respectability, and little dreamed of the
honors with which they were finally crowned. Mr. Osborn, therefore, could have had no selfish inducement to
contest the claim of Mr. Garrison, while either of them
would doubtless have been glad to know that the other
had avowed this sound and saving principle.

Before leaving this branch of my subject, I must notice
the surprising effort of Oliver Johnson to dispose of the
evidence I have submitted. He asserts that if the doctrine
in question had been proclaimed at the time mentioned
" it would not have failed to arrest public attention, and
throw a broad light over the whole country." When it
was announced by Garrison, he says, " it was like a re-

volving light on a headland, casting its rays afar over the raging sea." He says "the whole land was startled into attention ; the slave-holders were alarmed, and thenceforth had no peace," and that "it is morally certain that it would have been so in Tennessee if that light had been kindled there." My reply is that I am debating a question of fact, and, having conclusively shown that Mr. Osborn *did* proclaim this doctrine in 1814, the question about the consequences which Mr. Johnson says would have followed concerns him quite as much as me. But I will meet his argument directly, and expose its complete fallacy. This fallacy is found in the unwarranted assumption that public opinion in the South was as intolerant and inflammable in 1814 as it became in 1830 and the following years. This is notoriously not the fact, and it is marvelous that one so familiar with anti-slavery history as Mr. Johnson did not remember it. John Rankin is my authority for the statement that while he was a young man a majority of the people of east Tennessee were abolitionists, and I have already quoted his testimony that he afterwards preached immediate emancipation to large congregations in Kentucky. His brother, in a recent letter to me, confirms this testimony, and says that he frequently supplied a bookseller in Maysville, Kentucky, with copies of John Rankin's radical book already referred to, and that the State Abolition Society favored immediate emancipation. I have already quoted from articles in Lundy's *Genius* for 1825 and 1826 in favor of immediate emancipation, and I think no mob followed their publication. In 1826 the American convention for the abolition of slavery was held in Baltimore, representing 81 societies, 71 of which were in the slave States.[1] In 1827 there were 130 abolition societies in the United States, of which 106 were in the slave-hold-

---

[1] Wilson's Rise and Fall of the Slave Power, page 170.

ing States, and only 4 in New England and New York. Of these societies, 8 were in Virginia, 11 in Maryland, 2 in Delaware, 2 in the District of Columbia, 8 in Kentucky, 25 in Tennessee, and 50 in North Carolina.[1] These societies were no doubt largely the result of the labors of such men as Charles Osborn and Benjamin Lundy. Anti-slavery feeling was widely diffused, and although it was not very intense, and the subject of slavery was discussed without passion, the people seemed to be honestly in search of some method of escape from its evils. These historic facts show why it was that from 1814 to 1830 the proclamation of immediate emancipation failed to startle the country. It was the Southampton Insurrection of Nat. Turner, in Virginia, in 1831, and indications of insurrections in other States the same year, which fired the Southern heart, swept these societies out of existence, and inaugurated "the reign of terror" in the South which lasted till its overthrow by the power of war. Then it was that the battle-cry of immediate emancipation became the trumpet of alarm, and signalized the advent of the irrepressible conflict. In Mr. Garrison the word became flesh, for the nation was entering upon a new dispensation, and the hour and the man had met. Samuel Adams preached independence many years before it electrified the colonies. He was the real father of the revolution; but he was obliged to bide his time till the multiplying exactions of the mother country finally prepared the people for the conflict, and to write on their banners that "Taxation without representation is tyranny." No man is strong enough to wrestle with the logic of events.

I come now to the proof of my statement that Mr. Osborn edited and published the first anti-slavery newspaper in the United States, and is thus further entitled to the honor

---

[1] Poole's Anti-Slavery Opinions before 1800, page 72.

of being counted the pioneer of latter-day abolitionism. My task will not be difficult, and it will supply some corroborative proof of his anti-slavery position. We have seen that he removed to Mount Pleasant, Ohio, in 1816. In that year he issued his prospectus for a weekly newspaper to be called the *Philanthropist*, and published at that place; and on the twenty-ninth of August, 1817, the first number was issued. Its publication was continued till the eighth of October, 1818. The tone of the paper was earnestly moral and religious. He devoted its columns considerably to the interests of temperance and peace, but the burden and travail of his heart was slavery. I speak by authority, having the bound volumes of the paper before me. It was just such a paper as Elijah P. Lovejoy was murdered for publishing in Illinois twenty years later. Benjamin Lundy, then residing at St. Clairsville, was one of its agents, as the paper shows. The subject of slavery is discussed from eighty to ninety times, making an average of nearly twice in each weekly number. It was in the beginning of this year that the American Colonization Society was organized, with its headquarters at Washington, and the several anti-slavery societies then existing in this region of Ohio were all in favor of colonization as a scheme of gradual emancipation, as were those throughout the country generally; but Mr. Osborn disagreed with them. He opposed the scheme in repeated editorials, but allowed both sides of the question to be heard. Various articles were admitted favoring the policy of gradual emancipation, but not a line was written by himself in its approval. The limits of this article will not permit numerous or lengthy quotations from the paper, but I offer a few as specimens of its general character, beginning with the editorials. On page 44 of the first volume is the following on colonization:

"Without in anywise wishing to forestall public opinion,

or give a bias against the intentions of the American Colonization Society, the editor has great doubts of the justice of the plans proposed. It appears to him calculated to rivet closer the chains that already gall the sons of Africa, and to insure to the miserable objects of American cruelty a perpetuity of bondage. The free persons of color in the city of Philadelphia have protested against being sent back to a soil which separation and habit have combined to render disagreeable to them. The communication which follows is inserted because the author's intention is believed to be good, and because every investigation of the subject will tend to open the eyes of the public to the situation of this people. Those who have traveled through the Southern States, and observed the ignorance and vice with which slavery has enveloped the children of Africa, can hardly be persuaded that they are now fit instruments for propagating the Gospel."

On page 37 is the following:

"A correspondent says the coast of Africa has been robbed of its natives, who have with their sweat and blood manured and fertilized the soil of America. If their descendants are now (by way of reparation) to be forced back to that country, whose customs and whose soil are equally repugnant to them—query, are the thieves or the restorers most justifiable?"

In the second volume, on page 69, is a strong editorial on the slave trade and slavery. After referring to the action of England and Spain in dealing with this subject, it concludes:

" But much remains to be done. The system of slavery is acknowledged on all hands to be an evil of the greatest magnitude ; and it will require a degree of energy commensurate with the effects it has upon society to counteract its baleful influence, and now is the time for the advocates of freedom to exert themselves to overthrow that colossal fabric of despotism. Let the enlightened philanthropists of either hemisphere continue to carry on the benevolent work until they have finally accomplished the same, and receive the just reward of their labors, the grateful acknowledgements of millions of their fellow-mortals, whom they behold emerging from the gloomy caverns of despair and assuming the rank among the sons and daughters of men to which they are entitled by the laws of nature. In the language of one of the greatest orators of the present day, they will then have the satisfaction to know that through their instrumentality a large portion of their fellow-creatures are, politically speaking, 'redeemed, regenerated, and disenthralled by the Genius of Universal Emancipation.'"

It will occur to the reader as altogether probable that the name of Lundy's paper, which was started several years afterward, was suggested to him by this editorial. I quote the following from the editorial columns on page 154:

"A planter in the upper part of Georgia went down to Charleston to purchase slaves. A cargo had just been landed. They were set up at auction, declared to be sound in wind and limb, and were struck off to the highest bidder. This planter purchased his complement, and the driver conducted them off. On the way to Augusta one of the women accidentally saw the man who had been her husband in Africa. The dissevered pair immediately recognized each other, and their feelings at this unexpected meeting may be conceived by those who are acquainted with conjugal affection. The owner of the husband was moved at the scene, and proposed either to sell or buy, that the poor creatures might live together on the same plantation; but the other, hard-hearted man, would do neither. They, of course, were soon parted; the woman was conducted up the country, and soon after died of grief."

This is one of sundry articles on the same subject depicting acts of cruelty similar to those with which every reader of Uncle Tom's Cabin is familiar. In the same volume, on page 181, is an able and thorough article on colonization, from which I make brief extracts:

"On entering into this investigation we should bear in mind that we have long been called upon (and the present moment calls loudly) to cease to violate the laws of God and nature in holding our fellowmen in a state of bondage. It is the *slaves* who are suffering the most consummate misery, and it is the melioration of *their* condition which demands our first attention. Whatever laudable schemes may be formed for promoting civilization on the continent of Africa, or whatever benevolent designs may be entertained for the benefit of the free people of color on this side of the Atlantic, or whether these enterprises are directed by a sound or a visionary philosophy, it is not my present purpose to inquire. The great object still is to devise some system by which *slavery* may ultimately be terminated. If African colonization is not directed to this object, or capable of effecting it, we are still left to find some other expedient."

The article then proceeds to show, by facts and figures, the utter impracticability of the colonization scheme, and concludes:

"It is true that the plan might produce one very striking effect—it might amuse our minds with the mistaken idea of doing something valuable, until that Almighty Being who observes the conduct of nations and of individuals may in his wisdom and justice deprive us of the opportunity of being the instruments in so laudable a reformation by taking the great work into his own hands. And here my mind is forcibly struck with the sentiment of one of our greatest men: 'When I reflect that God is just, and that his justice can not sleep forever, I tremble for the fate of my country.'"

These samples will indicate the decided anti-slavery character of the paper, while its communications and selected matter will make this equally evident. The first issue contains three selections, one of which, being very brief, I quote:

"'I am astonished,' said an intelligent Turk, 'that the Americans should send a fleet to compel the surrender of slaves in our possession, when, in their own country, they keep thousands of Africans in bondage. They had better clean their hands before they lift them toward heaven.'"

On page 18 is an earnest letter on slavery from Anthony Benezett. On page 32 is an address from a member of the North Carolina Manumission Society, of the most radically anti-slavery type. On page 35 is an obituary notice of Paul Cuffe, a successful colored merchant and a man of signal benevolence and enterprise among his race. On page 37 is a strong article, probably written by Benjamin Lundy, over the signature of *Philo Justicia*, and a capital letter from Joseph Doddridge, from which I quote the following:

"Can we charge the most sore-handed despotisms in existence with anything worse than the personal slavery of the African race in our country? No! Even in the piratical states of the Barbary coast, if the Christian slave turns Musselman, he is free. Amongst us, if the slave becomes a Christian brother, he, nevertheless, still remains a slave."

Passing several brief articles, we find on page 76 the beginning of a lengthy one, by an intelligent colored man named William Blackmore, who discusses the question with considerable ability. In the course of it, in referring to the enemies of his race and their tribulations in the dying hour, he frames for them the following prayer:

"Almighty and incomprehensible Being! Thou knowest a part of Thy creation, the negroes and molattoes, have long been objects of our contempt; and we have even until this day been occasionally tormented with a sight of their black faces. We have seen many of them in the slave states stripped of every comfort of life, destitute of friends, and knowing not where to flee for succor and safety, and in this deplorable condition we passed by and left them, supposing their complicated sufferings would soon push them out of existence; but Thou didst put it into the hearts of Thy Samaritans to bring these wretched outcasts into this great inn which we inhabit, and to administer to their necessities. With the assistance of our ally, *Prejudice*, we thought before this to have convinced the world that they were made of more base material than we white people; but Thy great Apostle Paul declared that Thou hast 'made of one blood all nations of men.' We have long insisted that their color was a sufficient proof that they are of a distinct race greatly inferior to us; but Thou hast permitted Blumenbach, Smith and others to write so wisely upon the subject that many of the white people themselves now begin to think that climate, state of society, manner of living, etc., have produced the external differences which are apparent between them and us. We have contended again that the negroes are very deficient in point of intellect; but Thou hast suffered it to enter into the hearts of some of Thy believers to give some of them literary knowledge, and so we are likely to be overset in this our favorite hypothesis. We thought because we had the power it would be well enough to take away from them their natural, inherent and unalienable rights and privileges; but Thou hast put it into the hearts of certain persons in this state to think that we ought to do unto all men as we would wish them to do unto us.

" Now we are summoned to give up our stewardship, and seeing that we have not succeeded in our attempts to wrest Thy attributes out of Thy hands; and fearing from Thy many gracious promises and declarations in their favor that some of this despised people have been admitted into the mansions of Thy everlasting rest; we therefore humbly pray Thee that Thou will be graciously pleased to cast their black souls out of heaven before our spirits reach there; for it has been much against our will to dwell amongst them the few days of this life; and how can we bear the idea of being confined among them to all eternity?"

The following is from the *Chester and Delaware Federalist*, quoted on page 113:

"All is still as the grave. We boast that ours is the land of freedom. Here liberty dwells; this is the spot where the sacred tree flourishes, spreading its branches east and west, shading, protecting, the whole land. Our constitution solemnly declares that all men are born equally free. The enslaved and oppressed of Europe are welcomed to our shores as an asylum from oppression. We rub our hands and congratulate one another that we are the most free people on earth. Gracious heavens! and is it yet true that more than twelve hundred thousand of our fellow-creatures are doomed, themselves and their posterity, to hopeless bondage? Where are our abolition societies? Are they weary in well-doing? Where are those intelligent, ardent, benevolent men who exist in every country, who step forward on great occasions, animate their fellow-men to exertion, and direct their efforts to the attainment of noble ends? Are the spirits of Wilberforce, Clarkson and Benezett extinct? Or is it true that nothing can be done? *No—nothing can be done!* Go home and repose on your pillows of down; sleep away your lives in indolence and ease; and let the expression—nothing can be done—satisfy your consciences. Let the husband be separated from his wife, the mother from her little ones. Let the poor slave toil in hopeless misery, and bleed beneath the lash of his taskmaster. It will be useless to disturb Congress with your petitions—*nothing can be done.*"

On page 169 is an article by " E. B.," a Virginian, which ably discusses the question both in its political and moral aspects. I quote:

"It is not only absolutely *right* to devise some remedy for this evil, but it is absolutely necessary. We have shut our eyes and stopped our ears too long. Can we continue indifferent on so momentous a subject? We are called upon by honor, morality, and religion—by love for our country, ourselves, and our children. Let us not disregard these sacred obligations, but let us enter into a thorough investigation of the subject. Let us unite into select societies for the purpose of digesting a plan for the removal of this enormous evil, and, thus united in order and co-operating under the ties of virtue, honor, and love of our country, the difficulties attendant upon the subject will vanish before the wisdom of the nation. * * * It is impossible that one man should be the property of another. The master can not derive his claim of property from the law of nature, because by that law all men are equally free and independent. He can not derive it from the principles of civil government, for government was instituted for the common benefit, protection, and security of the community, and, when properly supported, admits no man or set of men to the possession of exclusive privileges. He can not refer to contracts with individuals, nor to conveyances from parents for their children, for no one will pretend to the existence of such contracts, and their validity could not be supported if they really existed. It can not be rested upon law, for such a law must be, technically speaking, unconstitutional. The constitution defines the object of government and the rights of individuals. These form barriers which legislation can never pass. It may, therefore, be boldly affirmed that slaves are not property.

They are injured human beings, whose sufferings call loudly for redress."

Mr. Osborn was one of the very first men of this country to oppose the use of slave-grown produce, and he continued personally faithful to this principle during his life; while the *Philanthropist* is clearly one of the first newspapers in the United States which espoused this duty. From an article copied from the Westchester *Recorder*, on page 174, I quote the following in reference to the slave trade:

"This great fountain of human blood that has been flowing on the continent of Africa for ages, whose streams have stained the shores of America and the West Indies, is kept in motion and supported by the consumers of the proceeds of slavery. They are the subscribers that furnish the fund by which the whole business is carried on. A merchant who loads his vessel in the West Indies with the proceeds of slavery does nearly as much at helping forward the slave trade as he that loads his vessel in Africa with slaves. They are both twisting the rope at different ends. * * * It is something paradoxical that a man will refuse to buy a stolen sheep, or to eat a piece of one that is stolen, and should not have the same scruples respecting a stolen man."

But I need not multiply these extracts, which I have given merely as illustrations of the spirit and make-up of the paper. I must not fail to mention, however, a very able and eloquent oration on slavery, by Thomas H. Genin, delivered at Mount Pleasant, Ohio, on the 18th of May, 1818, which is printed in the second volume, beginning on page 77. Mr. Genin came from New York to Ohio the year before, and was the intimate friend of Mr. Osborn. He also shared the friendship of Charles Hammond, Benjamin Lundy and De Witt Clinton. He had considerable literary gifts, and was the correspondent of Henry Clay and John Quincy Adams; and, although the rhetoric of his oration is a little florid, he discusses the slavery question with great thoroughness, and evinces a surprising insight into the nature and working of the institution. All the arguments and sophisms of the slaveholders with which the country has been familiar in later times are taken up and disposed of in this effort of more than seventy years ago as if he had been in the midst of the great conflict which so long afterward stirred the blood of both sections of the Union. The speech is prophetic, and deserves to be preserved as a choice relic of the literature of abolitionism in its pioneer days. Let me add, that I find scattered through the pages of the *Philanthropist* frequent selections of anti-slavery poems from Cowper, Shenstone, Montgomery and others, and I entertain no doubt whatever that its anti-slavery character is quite as clearly defined and uncompromising in tone as Lundy's *Genius of Universal Emancipation*, or James G. Birney's *Philanthropist*, published in Cincinnati in later years.

The priority of Mr. Osborn in the establishment of this paper has already been shown. He sold his establishment to Elisha Bates, and not to Elihu Embree, as Mr. Greely states in his "Conflict"; and Lundy, not liking the anti-slavery character of the paper under his management, as he declares in his account of these matters, began the publication, at Mount Pleasant, of the *Genius of Universal Emancipation*, in January, 1821, being three years and a half after the issue of the first number of the *Philanthropist*. These facts are given in "The Life of Benjamin Lundy," compiled by Thomas Earle, and published in 1847. We there learn, on the authority of Lundy, in speaking of the previous establishment of the *Philanthropist*, that "proposals were issued by Charles Osborn for publishing a paper at Mount Pleasant, to be entitled the *Philanthropist*. He stated in his prospectus that he should discuss the subject of slavery in the columns of the paper. The idea now occurred to me that I might act efficiently for the cause of emancipation—that I could select articles (for I did not think of writing myself) and have them published in the *Philanthropist,* and that I could also get subscribers to the publication. Engrossed with these thoughts, I went to work with alacrity. My leisure moments were now fully employed. When I sent my selections to Charles, I sometimes wrote him a few lines. After he had published the *Philanthropist* a few months, I was surprised at receiving from him a request that I should assist in editing it. The thought that I could do such a thing had not then even occurred to me. But on his repeating the request I consented to try, and from that moment, whenever I have thought that something ought to be done, my maxim has been, though doubtful of my ability, *try.* Although I resided ten miles from the office, and was extensively engaged in other business, I continued for some time to write editorial articles for the paper. At length Charles proposed to me to join him in the printing business, and to take upon myself the superintendency of the office. After some deliberation I consented to accept the offer." It seems, however, from the narrative, that Lundy never joined Osborn in the printing business, owing to circumstances which soon after drew him to Missouri, and that his only connection with the *Philanthropist* was that of an agent for the paper, and the writer of occasional articles over fictitious signatures. He had nothing to do with originating it, or superintending its management, and acted solely in the capacity of a subordinate, and a diffident, but sympathetic and faithful, disciple; and on his own showing the establishment of the the *Genius of Universal Emancipation* would never have been attempted if Mr. Osborn's successor had maintained the anti-slavery character of the *Philanthropist* under its previous management, when Lundy himself was its agent and zealous friend. He is, therefore, himself my witness that the honor now so generally claimed for him of being the first of our anti-slavery pioneers is altogether unwarranted by facts.

I have thus demonstrated my proposition that Charles Osborn was the first to proclaim the doctrine of immediate and unconditional emancipation, and that he, and not Lundy, became the pioneer of modern abolitionism by editing and publishing the first anti-slavery paper in the United States. On these points history has been made to bear false witness, and its record should be corrected. This correction will not pluck a single laurel from the saintly brow of Benjamin Lundy. It will be his imperishable honor that in his youth he surrendered a lucrative business and the sweet joys of home at the bidding of his conscience, and made himself a wanderer on the earth in the effort to rouse the consciences of men to the sin of slavery. His devotion to humanity was a divine fascination, and he literally gave up all for the slave. He is also entitled to the signal honor, as Oliver Johnson says, of " putting the burning torch of liberty into the hands of the man raised up by Providence to lead the new crusade against the slave power"; but Mr. Osborn kindled the blaze which lighted this torch of his Quaker disciple. When Lundy afterward met Garrison in Boston, in 1828, Mr. Osborn was his reference; and in 1847, when Mr. Garrison, in Cleveland, Ohio, met a son of Mr. Osborn, who still survives, he said to him: "Charles Osborn is the father of all of us abolitionists." He was, in fact, the real germ of the grand movement that drew into its service so many heroes and martyrs as it advanced, and finally swept slavery from the land, just as the quiet lakelet at the head of the Mississippi is the source of the great river which is swelled by its tributaries till lost in the gulf. Nor can the claim thus made weaken in any degree the historic position of Mr. Garrison as the moral hero of the movement. His indebtedness to Lundy he always frankly acknowledged; and, if the doctrine of immediate and unconditional emancipation was announced by others while he was a school-boy, it can not be set down to his discredit, nor does it follow, by any means, that he borrowed it from anyone. I believe it was the inevitable outcropping of his moral constitution, and came to him with the authority of a divine command. He did not need to take it at second-hand, while his overmastering personality popularized it, and imparted to it a meaning and power which quite naturally won for him the honor of its paternity.

In justice to my subject, I must not conclude this article without a brief reference to the controversy already alluded to, in which Mr. Osborn became involved in his later life with the society in which he had so long been a prominent member. In dealing with this subject, I shall speak plainly, but in no unfriendly spirit, respecting this most comely and praiseworthy body of religionists. Of Quaker parentage and training myself, my predilections incline me strongly in their favor. During my protracted connection with anti-slavery politics in one of the strongholds of these people in eastern Indiana, they were unitedly and earnestly my friends, and in what I shall now say I am conscious of no other motive than the service of the truth.

The year after Mr. Osborn sold his newspaper establishment he removed to Indiana. Several considerations induced him to abandon the publication of his paper. He desired to go further west, where his small resources would enable him to procure land for his children. He also felt that the influence of his paper was seriously thwarted by the mischievous and unmanageable scheme of colonization; while he believed he could more effectively serve the cause of freedom in the wider field of the traveling ministry, in which Woolman had labored with such remarkable results. In 1832, when the anti-slavery agitation had reached its fervent heat under the inspiration and leadership of Garrison, Mr. Osborn gave his heart to the work with renewed zeal. While in England in that year he met Elliot Cresson, an agent of the American Colonization Society, who begged him not to say anything that would hinder the raising of funds in aid of its work; but Mr. Osborn replied that he would not cease to expose its evil designs at home and abroad, and he made Cresson's mission a failure. His anti-slavery zeal fully kept pace with the multiplying aggressions of slavery, and, in the winter of 1839, he visited the eastern states, where he found the dominating influences among Friends decidedly opposed to his testimonies, and inclined to keep him silent, but he would not be fettered, and spoke out his whole mind freely. Some of his sermons were reported for the anti-slavery newspapers, and these lines of Whittier, inspired by a similar circumstance, were quoted as fitly applying to this intrepid assertion of the right of free speech:

> "Thank God for the token! one lip is still free
> One spirit untrammeled, unbending one knee;
> Like the oak of the mountain, deep-rooted and firm,
> Erect when the multitude bend to the storm;
> When traitors to freedom, and honor, and God,
> Are bowed at an idol polluted with blood;
> When the recreant North has forgotten her trust,
> And the life of her honor is low in the dust—
> Thank God that one arm from the shackles has broken!
> Thank God that one man as a *free-man* has spoken!"

On his return to the west he found that the ruling spirits in the Indiana Yearly Meeting had also taken a very decided stand against the abolitionists. The colonization members of the society, by some strange and unaccountable means, had gained the ascendancy over its anti-slavery members, and he was greatly troubled in mind respecting the situation in which he found himself placed. In the year 1841 the Indiana Yearly Meeting sanctioned a letter of advice which had been previously issued by the meeting for sufferings to its monthly and quarterly meetings, forbidding the use of their meeting-houses for anti-slavery lectures, and the joining in anti-slavery organizations "with those who do not profess to wait for Divine direction in such important concerns." The meeting also advised against anti-slavery publications by Friends without first submitting them to "the examination of a meeting for sufferings." This advice was unauthorized by the discipline of the society, and directly opposed to the well-known practice of Friends on both sides of the Atlantic. It showed that the power of slavery, which had taken captive over religious denominations throughout the country, had at last crept into the society, and was dictating its action. Charles Osborn was then a member of the meeting for sufferings, which is a delegated body in the society acting under appointment, like a committee, to transact important business in the interim of the regular sessions of the Yearly Meeting; and he and seven other anti-slavery members occupying the same position declined to obey this prohibitory advice. In doing so they justified themselves by the discipline and usages of the society and its well-known testimonies against slavery. They felt imperatively bound by their consciences to take this course, and that to do otherwise would be to recognize the infallibility of the Yearly Meeting and its right to bind them in all cases whatsoever. For this action these eight members were summarily removed from their positions as "disqualified," and their places filled by those who were willing to become the instruments of the Yearly Meeting in its warfare against the abolitionists.

What was to be done? These men had not violated the discipline of the society, or gone counter to any of its recognized practices and testimonies. They were not accused of any unsoundness in doctrine; and yet, without any formal charges of misconduct in any particular, and by an act of wanton usurpation, they were degraded from the places they had held. They begged that the reasons for this action might be spread upon the minutes as a matter of simple justice to themselves, and in order that they might not stand recorded as transgressors, and Mr. Osborn pleaded for this in a speech of much power and full of pathos and tenderness; but this petition was disregarded, and the perfectly unprecedented and arbitrary proceeding was carried out. If they submitted to this act of despotism they would be sharers in the apostacy of the society from its testimonies, and fellow-laborers with it against the slave. If they persisted in their disobedience they would, of course, be disowned for thus obeying their own consciences. They saw but one honorable or decent alternative. As lovers of the Society of Friends, and sincere believers in its doctrines and discipline, they could go out of the body which had cast them off for their anti-slavery principles and violated its discipline for that purpose, and organize a society of their own, with its machinery of monthly, quarterly and yearly meetings, and free from all pro-slavery domination. This they did, styling themselves the Society of Anti-Slavery Friends. They were driven out of the old body for their abolitionism, and Charles Osborn was spoken of as " gone, fallen, and out of the life," for no other cause. This occurred in 1842, at the yearly meeting which gave Henry Clay, the owner of fifty slaves and president of the American Colonization Society, a seat among the ruling elders, and who, in a public speech the day before, had declared that " the slaves must be prepared for freedom before they can receive that great boon," and that "the Society of Friends take the right stand in relation to this subject." History was thus repeating the old story of "Pilate and Herod friends," and illustrating the desire of the society, as expressed by its meeting for sufferings in 1841, to "retain the place and influence" which it had "heretofore had with the rulers of our land." There was a peculiar sting in the saying of Mr. Osborn afterward that these Friends "deemed it a departure from the well-known principles of the society to do anything in the anti-slavery cause without a divine impulse and clear opening in the light of truth leading thereto; but for their opposition to the abolitionists they had no impulse, no opening, to wait for."

It will probably be news to thousands that the Quakers thus succumbed to the power of slavery; but such is the melancholy fact, and they have no right to "escape history." Among the rank and file of the body in Indiana there were doubtless very many true anti-slavery men; but at the time of which I speak the chief rulers believed in colonization and gradual emancipation. They took special pains, in dealing with legislative bodies, slave-holders and the public, to inform them that they had no connection, in any way, with abolitionism. They so assured Henry Clay while in Richmond. Leading members frequently reiterated the charge that abolitionists had "put back the cause of emancipation"; and some of them insisted that aiding slaves on their way to Canada involved men in the crime of man-stealing. Many of the rulers of the denomination in the eastern, as well as the western, States had "their ears filled with cotton." They discoursed very piously about the attempt of abolitionists "to abolish slavery in their own strength," and argued that paying men for anti-slavery lectures was opposed to the Quaker testimony against a "hireling ministry." Ministers, elders and overseers, took the lead in these reactionary proceedings;

and it was one of the curiosities of human nature to find the followers of John Woolman and Anthony Benezett laboring with their brethren for attending anti-slavery meetings, closing the doors of their churches against anti-slavery lectures, and setting up a system of espionage over the publication of anti-slavery articles by members of the society. Such men as Isaac T. Hopper, among the Hicksite Friends, and Arnold Buffum, among the Orthodox, were disowned for their fidelity to the slave. This work of proscription was generally based upon some false pretense, as was the fact in the case of Mr. Buffum. In dealing with Mr. Osborn and his associates, the Indiana yearly meeting did its best to cover up the ugly fact that they were degraded on account of their anti-slavery principles. With great dexterity in the use of scripture, much circumlocution, and a cunning and tergiversation that would have won the heart of Talleyrand or Loyola, they played their game of ecclesiastical tyranny; but the facts of the transaction, as now seen in the clear perspective of history, leave them perfectly unmasked. I have carefully examined the documents and papers pertaining to the controversy on both sides, and speak from the record. Strange as it may seem, the claims of justice were so completely subordinated to the peace and unity of the society that even a deputation of English Friends, who came over as mediators in this trouble, utterly refused to look into the merits of the controversy, and insisted upon the unconditional return of the seceding members to the body which had so flagrantly trampled upon their rights. Humanity was forgotten in the service of a sect, and Quakerism itself disowned by its priesthood.

But the anti-slavery movement took an unexpected turn. The annexation of Texas and the war with Mexico roused the country, and poured a flood of light on the character and designs of the slave-holding interest. The anti-slavery agitation of 1848 and the passage of the Fugitive Slave Act of 1850 brought large reinforcements to the cause of freedom. The repeal of the Missouri Compromise and the struggle to make Kansas a slave State still further enlightened the people. The dullest scholars began to get their lessons. Slave-holding madness so anointed the eyes of the people that the cloven feet of abolitionism disappeared, and the Quakers, like other religious bodies, began to take a new view of their duties. "The world," on which they turned their backs in 1841 to avoid its "contamination," had at last taught them more wisdom than any "divine impulse" had ever been able to impart. They became themselves abolitionists, and gloried in the very cause which provoked their contempt during the ugly apostasy they had parenthesized into the beautiful anti-slavery record of the sect.

But did they do justice to the men they had persecuted for righteousness' sake? Did they make any official acknowledgement of the wrong they had done, as did other religious denominations in like cases? No. Individual members solicited the seceders to return to the fold. They said to them, "Come back to us! No questions will be asked, and no conditions exacted. Make no disturbance, but come and go with us." Most of the seceders finally returned, but some of them demanded an amendment of the minutes of the society which should recognize the injustice done them for their anti-slavery fidelity. This was denied in all such cases, and they stand on the records as "disqualified" members. Charles Osborn died in 1850, a grieved and sorely-disappointed old man, and his grief would not have been assuaged if he could have foreseen the action of the society in refusing to correct its records after it had espoused the very principles for the advocacy of which he had been exiled from its bosom. Harshly and unjustly as he had been treated, he would scarcely have believed this possible. But the society was handicapped by its record. Much as it owed Mr. Osborn, morally and spiritually, its love of consistency and the cravenness of human nature triumphed over its conscience. It could not do him justice without condemning itself. It could not espouse his cause as a faithful minister of the Gospel and an anti-slavery prophet without advertising its recreancy to humanity and its injustice to a great-hearted and brave man.

But the friends of humanity, irrespective of sect or party, should join in fitly honoring him. During his life abolitionism was a despised thing. He did not live to see the glory which was so soon to come, nor anticipate its coming. As to his reputation, he took no thought for the morrow. The newspaper which proves his right to be ranked as the first of our anti-slavery pioneers seems only to have been preserved by an accident. The memory of other faithful pioneers has been carefully and lovingly guarded; but history has slighted his record, and liberty, in searching for her jewels, has strangely overlooked his name. Touched by these facts, and believing that "no power can die that ever wrought for truth," I have felt commanded to do my part in the work of adding a new star to the galaxy of freedom, a new name to the roll-call of reformers. If I have succeeded in any degree in this labor of love, I shall rejoice; but, in any event, I shall share the satisfaction which attends a sincere endeavor to serve the truth.

www.ingramcontent.com/pod-product-compliance
Lightning Source LLC
Chambersburg PA
CBHW030710110426
42739CB00031B/1680